Leisure Arts 45

Working with
Water-Solub
Pencils

Wendy Jelbert

SEARCH PRESS

Introduction

Water-soluble (or aquarelle) pencils, when used with inventive and imaginative techniques, can produce a wide range of exciting textures, patterns and effects. They really do deserve to be treated as a medium in their own right, rather than just as a substitute for other materials.

The technology involved in the manufacture of water-based media is so highly advanced that permanence is now virtually guaranteed, and more and more rich, varied colours, rivalling those of paints, are now available at quite competitive prices.

There are many makes on the market now, each manufacturer offering different qualities, such as harder or softer leads, different thicknesses, and, of course, each has its own range of colours.

As with most modern materials, these pencils can be bought separately, or in prepared boxes of twelve, twenty-four, thirty-six, forty-eight, and, in some cases, sixty or seventy-two. You can also buy a 'landscape' selection, or a collection intended for portraits. However, before investing in a whole set I suggest that it would be a good idea to try out some of the different types.

I did this and I soon realised just how versatile they are. They can be rubbed and smudged, and can be rubbed out, erased, or highlighted with a putty eraser if necessary. They can also be washed over with a soft brush loaded with water. Alternatively, I found I could wash them from the tip with a brush and deposit them on the paper.

Pencils are easily portable and are excellent for detailed work on carefully observed studies of flowers or animals *in situ*, without the pressures and problems of quick-drying washes!

Alternatively, if you are a landscape painter, you can block in larger areas using a pencil-tip wash, or make accurate colour sketches on the spot, to be worked up in the studio later on.

You will need to invest some time and effort in practising with these materials; as you will discover, the more you experiment, the more will be revealed. You will probably find that water-soluble pencils will perform best when taken beyond conventional channels, when you exploit their free-flowing colour qualities by using water with a brush or a spray, rather than relying on them purely as drawing instruments.

Pansy.

A scene of a Cornish granite farm depicting an assortment of textures, and leaving some of the white paper untouched for the geese shapes.

If you make mistakes when using pencils, these can be erased with a putty eraser only when in the form of a drawing, because once you add the water, the paper absorbs the pigment. You can use this method to gain highlights or to diffuse hard edges.

Most papers, such as cartridge or thin sketch-book paper, can be used, especially when you are not working with water. Once wetted, a thin paper will wrinkle and be in danger of being punctured, especially by a hard pencil, so my personal choice would be a 190gsm (90lb) or 300gsm (140lb) watercolour Not surface.

Study in aquarelle graphite pencil.

Sketching and drawing

In making a drawing or study from any object, the mind may be influenced by two factors: first, the endeavour to produce an exact likeness, resembling a photograph; second, the desire to make a judicious selection, and to put down your own personal poetic thoughts on the matter on to paper. Equally, the recording of facts and details is extremely important for future reference, as are the feelings the subject aroused in the first place. Both these requirements can sometimes conflict in the same drawing. For this reason, I often draw and sketch the subject several times, stating different things about it. First of all, I may make a quick sketch capturing a brief moment or mood, and then I may take a photograph recording all the details (but in a sterile form!). Finally, if there is time, I will finish off with a detailed drawing in tone and texture.

On these and the following two pages I have sketched and drawn several subjects in this medium. Water-soluble pencils and aquarelle graphite pencils are ideal for the artist when speed and convenience are essential.

The various makes of graphite pencils are manufactured and available in small sets, or they can be bought individually. Easy to handle and light to carry, they can be used for sketching in many ways to gather important reference work, and can therefore be used with ease in your sketch-book. You can vary from a loose scribble, washed gently with water, thus dissolving it into soft washes, to bold vigorous statements which, when overlaid with additional layers of either dry or wetted pencils, can give excellent sketches or drawing impressions.

Note the effect of water on dry pencil worked with varying pressures to depict tonal changes.
Left: a water-soluble pencil (burnt sienna).
Right: an aquarelle graphite pencil (3B).

Harbour scene in water-soluble pencil.

The field gate.

In this sketch of the field gate, I drew in the main features and then, using hatched and textural markings, made impressions of the foliage and grasses, strengthening them with tones of the shadowed area before washing over the whole image with a soft brush and clean water. This diffused the hard edges and softened the darker tones.

When the paint was completely dry, I reinstated some of the more pronounced branches and details on the gate. I do like these mellow browns, which give such lovely earthy tones; and the soft browns and light reds, reminiscent of those used by the Old Masters, are excellent.

When using the pencils in a more traditional style, I am able to ring the changes by drawing with the dry pencil, as in the harbour scene on page 5, and then adding another dimension by adding water to the dry burnt-sienna image, such as the portrait of my student Phyllis (opposite).

The prelude to every successful painting is some kind of preliminary drawing. In the cat studies (opposite), which later on I worked into a painting, I endeavoured to jot down the expressive movements that animals make and which are almost impossible to capture when you are trying to get them down at speed. They really do seem to sense that they are being sketched, even when they appear to be fast asleep, and move just before you can complete the pose. The saying that you do not know a subject until you draw it is quite true.

Here, in these three quick studies, I used burnt sienna, violet and Vandyke brown pencils, both wet and dry, to get a varied quick and rugged line. I wet them only to give a brief tonal statement. The pencils also give a lovely 'flow' to a drawing, and an expressively lively line can be achieved by varying the pressure and choosing to have a wet or a dry finish.

Phyllis.

Three studies of cats using burnt sienna, violet and Vandyke brown pencils.

Trying out water-soluble pencils

Surprisingly, water-soluble pencils are often regarded as instruments for children alone. Through my years of experience as an art teacher, and as a demonstrator for several art manufacturers, I have discovered that they are a great asset to any painter (whether professional or amateur), designer, or illustrator. They offer great spontaneity and freedom of expression, whether used for drawing or for actually carrying the colour.

They can be used in an uncomplicated way, just as if you were using an ordinary graphite pencil, or can be mixed in with plain pencil. If colour is the main purpose, they may be used to indicate colour, either with feathery, delicate marks, or with watery washes encouraged from the pencil-markings themselves by using a simple pot-plant sprayer or a brush loaded with clean water.

These pencils need sympathetic handling, so their many qualities and great potential can be exploited to the full. This collection of exercises will help you on your way!

1. Try some scribbles of pencil, with a wash of clear water to dissolve the markings.

2. The same exercise as above but with a hatching of another colour.

3. The same again, but with a third colour added.

4. Draw a graded square of dry-pencil work, altering the pressure used and therefore varying the amount of pencil deposited on the paper, and then wet half the surface.

5. Make some small pencil stab marks, altering the texturing, and spotting in another colour. Try wetting half the paper beforehand, and watch the markings dissolve.

6. Set three colours up in strips and try wetting them and watching the mixtures of a fourth colour covering the lighter shade.

7. Holding three colours in the same hand at once, dot at different angles, spotting the surface, then wet over the top of the marks.

8. Repeat as above, but making little circles.

9. Gather a brush full of colour directly from the pencil-point, and discover how it resembles a true watercolour wash.

10. Experiment with the use of the pencil by rolling it and then dragging it over a dry and wetted surface.

11. Repeat as above, but using more colours.

12. With three pencils bunched together, doodle and wander around the paper in a dry manner.

13. Depositing a thick layer of pencil-work in the centre of your square, tease out the colour with a wetted brush.

14. Repeat as above, but using two colours and easing the colour together in the centre.

15. Arrange three blocks of colour in your square, dropping on a little clear water and rocking your paper slowly to reveal the way all the colours blend and fuse.

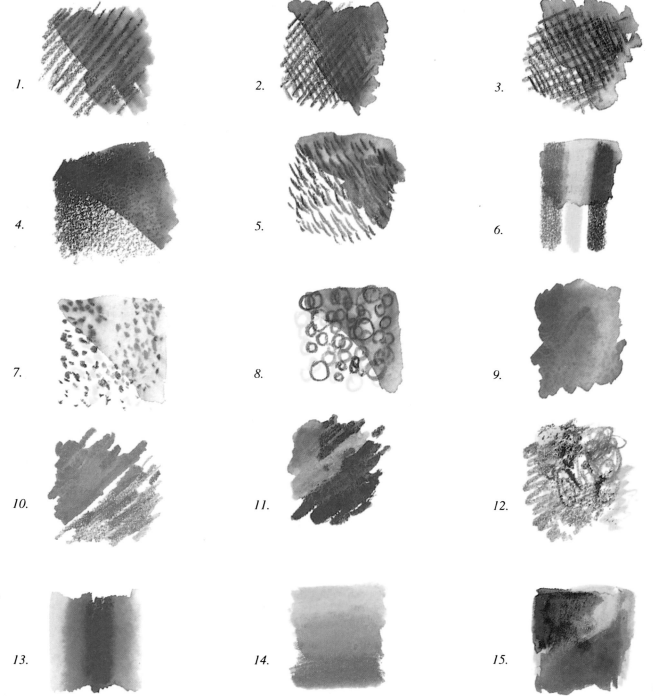

1.

2.

3.

4.

5.

6.

7.

8.

9.

10.

11.

12.

13.

14.

15.

Other techniques

When you have experimented with the previous exercises and have become accustomed to the characteristics of water-soluble pencils, it is time to go even further. There are endless combinations and additions, some of which are mentioned in this section. Many are yet to be discovered, and on this journey of exploration you will surely stumble on several of them yourself, widening and improving your artistic language.

There is no reason why any one of these media cannot be combined with watercolours, mixed with another water-soluble medium, used with masking fluid, or used in combination with various inks. Scoring the paper, either before or after the colour has been applied (when more colour is added the image is emphasised), or adding salts to the washes can also give interesting textural results.

On these pages I have again set out some suggestions for you to try.

1. Apply masking fluid using a drawing pen. When it is thoroughly dry, apply washes from the tips of the pencils. When the washes are dry, rub off the masking fluid to reveal the white paper which has been protected by the fluid.

2. This shows layers of wet colour from the pencil tips with wetted-pencil work applied on top. By trying various colours, you will find that some cover better than others.

3. Try out the same exercise as above, but using dry colours in assorted strokes.

4. Try mixtures of wet and dry pencil work, combined with ink, which is used to define the edges.

5. Use larger dry areas of pencil to cover a pencil-tip wash that has been allowed to dry.

6. Try developing an assortment of dry markings with pencils of different qualities and colours.

7. Drop some salt into a watercolour wash taken from the tip of the pencil. Allow this to dry, and then brush off briskly to reveal marbled or starred effects.

8. Here, watercolours are used as a base and then overlaid with pencil. Successive applications can be used for depth and texturing.

1.

2.

3.

4.

5.

6.

7.

8.

Exploring other techniques.

Trying out various methods and styles

In this fun section, I have used sweets as the basis for putting some of the previous exercises into practice. The key to getting good consistent results is knowing what to expect.

Materials

Aquarelle pencils in various colours.

Brushes and watercolour paper.

Ink and pen, or steel-nibbed pen.

Masking fluid and drawing pen.

Pot-plant sprayer.

Watercolours.

The yellow toffee

Dry-pencil work in bright yellow was cross-hatched in delicate strokes in the main area. For the deeper shades, I used additional layers in ochre, burnt sienna, and dark browns. This gentle use of layering of colours is an effective way of weaving rich colour and depth. By a change of grip and the use of differing amounts of pressure you can experiment with the broad range of effects. Light pressure creates gentle tones and allows more pencil to be added. Pressing harder adds a dense coating that will not accept many additional layers!

The green chocolate

I took a bright green wash from the pencil-tip with a soft brush and allowed it to dry. Then I added layers of pure dry colour, rather as I did in the above exercise, and hatched in some fine lines, allowing the initial coats to 'glow' through. Finally, I just suggested a shadow in light-blue and grey pencil-work.

The blue sweet

A wash of light bright-blue pencil was painted over the whole drawing and background. While it was still wet, I blocked in the small abstract shapes in different blues, capturing the shiny surface design. I left small slivers of untouched paper to serve as highlights.

When everything was dry, I applied some dry-pencil hatchings, and some ink to create the wrapping and shadow details.

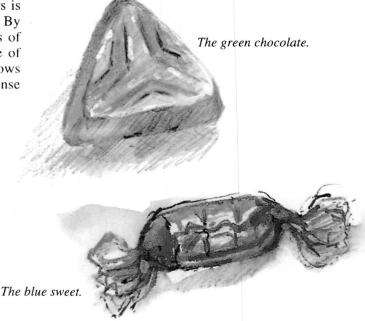

The green chocolate.

The yellow toffee.

The blue sweet.

The round blue sweet

I sketched in the shape with blue pencil and wetted the surface of the paper. Then I dotted brown and blue pencil-shavings into this and let them fuse and merge. The juxtaposition of diffused and sharp images offers an extremely attractive contrast.

The patterns on the wrapping were completed in dry-pencil drawing.

The milk chocolate

I cross-hatched and layered a variety of fine dry pencil lines in various browns over an initial undercoat of yellow-ochre watercolour, which was dry before I applied the lines.

The coloured drawing surface was then gently wetted with the small sprayer. Do take care not to 'blast' at your fragile image as it has the habit of quickly running off the page! You may need to have several goes before the results are acceptable.

The striped sweet

I drew in the sweet and then applied the white decorative lines using masking fluid and the ruling pen. When this was dry, I placed in the yellow foundation colour with the transparency of the pencil, using a wash directly from its tip. Take care when using masking fluid with direct pencil work, as you may lift the image beneath. Here I always use the colour with a brush.

After rubbing out the dried masking fluid, I cross-hatched a few yellow and burnt-sienna lines over some of the white lines to deepen the shadows. To complete the exercise, I applied a layer of blue wash to merge the colours into a flowing semi-transparent wash.

The striped sweet.

The round blue sweet.

The milk chocolate.

13

Mixing greens

Painting foliage and trees could take up a whole book in itself! In my art classes, every year, before venturing outside, we always have a basic lesson on the complex mixing of greens, and whatever stage a student seems to have achieved, everyone joins in. It is an endless source of study and a challenge to every artist.

The water-soluble pencils make perfect companions for outdoor work.

Colour chart

Here I have set out a simple chart, restricting the mixing of greens to a very easy-to-follow formula.

The squares in the left-hand column are each made up from a combination of a ready-made bright green and another colour, and worked with dry pencils. The second column of squares are similar combinations of colours that have been worked with water and a brush.

1. Grey plus a mid-toned brightish blue-green gives a cool, soft green.

2. Burnt sienna mixed with a strong mid green makes a bolder, useful mid-toned green.

3. A flesh colour combined with a yellowy mid green results in a delicate warm green.

4. A bright emerald green with violet gives a 'greyed' darker green.

5. Red and orange mixed with a mid-toned strong green makes a lovely warm autumnal green.

There really is a wonderful variety of greens available. Another good thing you could try is to use the same green throughout the whole exercise.

A combination of colours in short stabbing marks showing an assortment of greens, wet and dry.

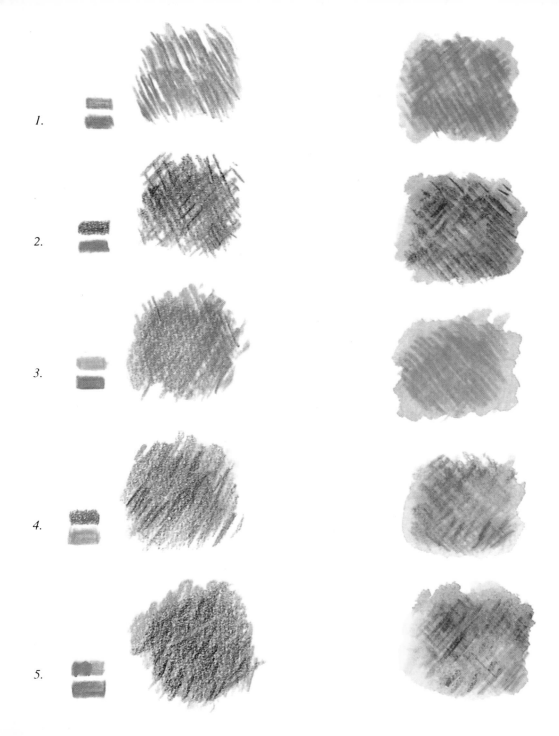

1.

2.

3.

4.

5.

15

*This tree study is from my sketchbook.
I used a combination of dry colour
work and some washes taken from the
pencil tip with a brush.*

16

Spiky.

Dotty.

Wavy.

Feathery.

Starry.

Foliage falls into distinctive groups.

Trees and foliage
Demonstration

When you are trying to convey the maximum effect of foliage, using line alone in the drawing will not provide sufficient information for the varied details of patterns and textures essential to portray each individual tree or plant. To conjure up the vast and expressive 'artistic vocabulary' needed to paint this subject, I suggest you acquaint yourself with a few of the assortment of leaves in your own garden. Place them on the table and study them carefully, noting the character of colour, pattern of leaf, and the massed effect of each. Above I have sorted out several types, using many different colours: blues, greens, violets, yellows, and browns. Although the subject is very complicated, I find that foliage falls into distinctive groups: dotty, wavy, feathery, starry, or spiky. By practising these massed effects, an impression of a particular type is quickly produced.

A tree is a beautiful but difficult subject. For this demonstration I chose one that offered a wide array of greens, textural properties and tones. I hope this exercise helps you produce a portrait of a tree for future reference.

Materials
Pencils: mid, bright and deep greens; deep violet; burnt sienna; orange; pale, dark and turquoise blues.

190gsm (90lb) watercolour paper.

Soft watercolour brush.

Stage 1
First I sketch in the main outlines and various negative shapes (shapes that the sky forms through the tree itself) and jot down some of the large branches, using my violet aquarelle pencil. With a ruling pen, I add a thin rendering of masking fluid (for the cow-parsley beneath the canopy of the tree), then some of the grasses, and the two large branches amid the tree mass.

Stage 1.

Stage 2.

I scribble in the main leafy areas of the tree using mid green, burnt sienna and violet. I then complete the stage by laying in a wash for the sky and the distant horizon, taking the colour from the tip of my pale-blue pencil.

Stage 2
Next I add a little orange and turquoise pencil to the grasses. With a generous wash of clear water loaded on my soft brush, I run the colours gently together over the whole tree and the surrounding area. When these have blended and dried slightly, I apply more colour to the surface, using dark blue and violet into the core of the tree and down into the roots and cow parsley, giving depth and shadows.

Stage 3
Now I intensify the darks within the tree, emphasising the shadows formed from the topmost branches, in a rhythmical action through the whole structure to its

very base. Then I tease out these areas into dry sweeps resembling soft leaves, fading into the sky, using burnt sienna and violet. I then rub off the masking fluid, displaying white markings for the grasses, branches and cow-parsley. I paint over the branches and some of the grasses, using pale yellow from the pencil tip and a soft brush. I then give depth to some of the cow-parsley with a little burnt sienna; I leave some of the white shapes, especially a few grasses and cow-parsley, for contrast.

I reload my brush with dark blue, and violet from the pencil tips, and paint into the tree centre for the final application of dark. Then I trail my burnt sienna, light green, and violet over the tree defining branches and twigs, bringing them beyond the tree's main outline to form a natural effect.

Finally I draw in more cow-parsley in dark pencil to add life and contrast to the area beneath the tree.

Stage 3.

19

A cockerel

Demonstration

I photographed this handsome bird while on an art trip to a local farm museum. As so many of my students had such a magical time painting the hens, geese and cockerels of all varieties, I thought you might like to have a go at the cockerel's colourful plumage.

Materials

Pencils: deep blue, cadmium/crimson reds, ochre, blue, deep charcoal, yellow, brown, pink.

Soft No. 6 watercolour brush.

190gsm (90lb) Not watercolour paper.

Stage 1

Here I quickly sketch in the brief details with a deep blue and softly block in layers of red for the comb, dark blue and deep charcoal for the legs, pink for the feet, and a mixture of yellow and ochre for the neck and beak.

Stage 2

I add a little background colour with deep charcoal, brown, and yellow, to give an impression of straw. Using my No. 6 soft brush with clear water, I diffuse the colours.

Stage 1.

Stage 2.

Stage 3.

Stage 3

While the paper is still wet, I reinforce some of the accents of dark tones of the legs, tail and body, as the wet pencils are at their darkest while fluid. The feathers need more attention, so I draw more tiny lines of feathers and texture over the body, feet, comb and beak. To complete the picture, I now brush on a wash of light blue from the tip of the pencil, applying it as a glaze over the background and the shadowed area cast in the foreground.

Seaside reflections

Demonstration

T his small seaside cameo is of my son Richard, many years ago. He is now twenty-four years old! I used a coloured photograph, which helped with the tones and important features such as the reflections. Do bear in mind that coloured photographs can be deceptive, so colour notes should be made at the same time if a special colour theme is to be remembered!

Materials
Pencils: ultramarine blue, burnt sienna, raw umber, orange, brown, mid violet, and dull mid green.

No. 6 watercolour brush.

Masking fluid and ruling pen.

Watercolour paper.

Stage 1.

Stage 1
First I pencil in the child and seaside setting, using my raw-umber pencil, then draw over the highlighted areas with the masking fluid, over his back and head, and over the small rocks and ripples in the pool.

Stage 2.

Stage 2
I loosely scribble in the background colours, using violet and dull green for the rocks and seaweedy pools, pressing heavily in order to deposit more colour, as these features are in the foreground. Raw umber, blue, and orange are blocked into the foreground pools and the impression of the reflection. I spend longer on the figure of the child, outlining the blue details on his garments, and filling in the flesh tones and hair with burnt sienna and raw umber, then taking down some of these colours into the reflections. Be careful not to lift the masking fluid underneath!

Stage 3
In this last stage, I add water over the whole picture with the brush, except in the area of light water on the left-hand side, to spread and dissolve the watercolour. Here and there I restate darker accents, using blue and brown straight into the wet wash, as in the rocks and reflections, details of the shadows on the legs, and folds in the clothing. After the picture has dried, I rub off the masking fluid and soften the white markings with pale blue painted from the tip of the pencil, applied with the brush.

To gain maximum effect from the colours, I glaze over the water with scribblings of blue and brown to give movement to the pool and draw in more rock textures in the foreground. Sharp and trailing lines in dry-pencil lines are added, to indicate the contours of the pools.

Stage 3.

The French balcony

This is a very detailed work using cerulean and ultramarine blues; vermilion; dark and light green cross-hatched with violet; yellows; and burnt sienna, in order to gain all the variety of greens needed in this picture. The pencil-work is mostly dry, giving an open-weave effect and letting the lightness of the paper show through the delicate pencil lines.

The foliage needed to be drawn in using many different markings, to make the plants varied and fascinating, as with the vines, fuchsias, and distant bushes. When some of these darks needed intensifying, I dipped the pencil into water (or my mouth!) and applied several layers of neat colour until I had the colour and strength required.

The shadows are gently drawn in with slanting markings close together, using violet, burnt sienna and blues, and making certain that they fall correctly along the ground, across the walls and along the steps. Note how the background made the foreground subjects 'glow' with the sunshine, or become darker and more intense with the deep shadows. It was this interplay of contrasting elements – the distance influencing the foreground subjects and the shapes of the long shadows across the balcony – that attracted me to this complicated but intimate scene.

The blue shutters

In this French scene I used water-soluble pencils *in situ*. The seperate stages are hard to define, and the picture was done very quickly in the hot sunshine! Everything seemed blue, and the colours of the shadows and the shutters went so well with the soft tissue-pink of the hollyhocks.

I drew in the preliminary details in blue, and then overdrew the canopy of vines, flowers, and foliage at the base of the vine. I blocked in the deeply shadowed area beneath the foliage, beneath the shutters and around the plants then briskly established the wall colour of the Naples yellow. To this I added small shavings from the blue pencil to add texture, and a ground covering of bright green with specks of blue and violet using the wash taken from the tips of my pencils.

Next I wet the whole space and outlined the highlighted areas with greens and blues; then I crudely hatched some ochres and pinks into the shadows. Finally, I used a steel-nibbed pen to define some of the branches and the details of the grass.

Polyanthus

I bought this delightful old teapot in a car-boot sale, and placed the brightly coloured polyanthus in it for my art class to paint. First of all I drew in the main proportions, the 'flow' of the foliage and the details on the teapot with a blue aquarelle pencil, and if you look closely at the completed work, you may see some of these lines, especially around the leaves and the pot.

I blocked in the dark background by cross-hatching with a combination of red, blue, green and violet. This shadowed area contrasted with the lovely light yellow-green of the top leaves.

Some of the foliage was scribbled in using yellow, blue and a little red. I tried to place some in slight shadow while the remainder caught the light. I also tried to capture the characteristic fleshy veins and the wrinkled surface of the leaves using deeper colours for the smaller veins and a cross-hatching of mid-green and blue for the wrinkles.

The bright-red flowers were a mixture of vermilion and crimson with a spot of yellow, for a realistic 'clash' of colours to make the flowers 'glow'. These contrasts are essential for the heads to look as thought they are growing naturally at various angles.

Still using the pencils dry, I continued to pencil in the structure of the pot by applying blue in varying degrees of thickness around the base, neck, handle, spout, and belly, to form an elegant shape. Note the contrast between the spout and handle and the background . . . dark against light.

I then drew the teapot's shadow in blue, violet and a little green. This emphasises the light-source coming from behind the pot and flowers. The shine on the table top was lightly drawn in using pale yellow.

Finally, I sketched in the pattern using all the previous colours but predominantly reds, making sure the details were accurately curving along the pot's surface and not looking flat and unnatural.

Farm cat in old barn window

I discovered this delightful scene in an old Cornish farmyard that had been painted long ago by the Newlyn artist Stanhope Forbes. It resembled a splendid time capsule containing a multitude of wonderful 'olde-worlde' farm scenes of geese, old barns, crumbling farm windows and doors, and ancient farm machinery half hidden in weeds and cobwebs.

This window really did have this cat sleepily watching me in the peeling blue frame. The dark, shadowy background contrasted beautifully with the broken wooden boards punctured with rusty nails, and the animal's light markings.

Over the whole surface of a canvas-marked watercolour paper I washed over a covering of yellow ochre, using a brush and taking the colour from the wetted tip of my water-soluble pencil, and then let this dry. I then drew in an initial sketch of the window and cat details, the layout of the blocks of granite, and the weeds sprouting from the surrounding window frame.

I cross-hatched raw- and burnt-sienna pencil-work over some of the walls to give a weathered effect and wet some of these for softness and contrast. In the variety of foliage I used a bright light green and drew in the dark shapes with wetted mid- and dark-green pencils for maximum depth.

For the shadows, I used dry dark-blue and brown pencils and sketched in the dark areas, allowing the warmth from the yellow-ochre initial wash to glow through.

I added the cat's markings with a small rigger brush and a wash from a mixture of black and brown pencils. Finally, I carefully drew in the details on the wooden planks, the grasses, and the rust stains, using dry mid-brown and light-red pencils.

Daffodils

There is nothing more refreshing and pleasing than gathering a bunch of crisp, delicately perfumed daffodils. Their bright, cheerful trumpets announce the return of spring, and I always feel that they resemble banners of hope for the year ahead after the dark, cold winter days.

Every spring term my art class asks to be allowed to paint daffodils, and it seems as if this habit is here to stay! There are always the same pitfalls, though: nature rarely supplies the perfect composition, so we have to compose it carefully for ourselves.

I used pencils in blues, burnt sienna, violet, bright and dark greens, orange, and browns. Several yellows, including cold ones and warm ones, plus yellow ochre and burnt sienna, were drawn in for the flower heads. I wet them for a freer wash and tightened them up with the details in violet and brown after the wash had dried.

Before starting on any subject, remember to make sure that you understand the influence of the background. The flowers are the colour and tone they are because of the background colour and tone. See how the dark accents behind the flower-heads highlight them and make their colour sing because of the colours chosen. The contrast of the light heads against a darker background (in the centre) and the darker ones against a lighter rendering (on the right) is an important thing to build into any flower picture to prevent the picture from being too much the same all over.

Note, too, that the glass container has areas of contrast, with the light rim and background, and the darker background which highlights the varying lines of light playing on the glass. The clear, sharp lines drawn by the pencils are ideal for this detail.

I have outlined several of the petals with the pencil and then washed over with bright yellow to 'bloom' the colour into the surrounding area in order to add interest.

First published in Great Britain 1995
Search Press Limited,
Wellwood, North Farm Road,
Tunbridge Wells, Kent TN2 3DR

ISBN 0 85532 791 X

Distributors to the art trade:

UK
Winsor & Newton,
Whitefriars Avenue, Wealdstone,
Harrow, Middlesex HA3 5RH

USA
ColArt Americas Inc.,
11 Constitution Avenue, P. O. Box 1396, Piscataway, NJ 08855-1396

Arthur Schwartz & Co.,
234 Meads Mountain Road, Woodstock,
NY 12498

Australia
Max A. Harrell
1357 Malvern Road, Malvern, Victoria 3144

New Zealand
Caldwell Wholesale Limited,
Wellington and Auckland

South Africa
Ashley & Radmore (Pty) Limited,
P. O. Box 2794, Johannesburg 2000

Note: The names of colours in this book are aproximate ones. Each manufacturer's products are slightly different in colour, and if a precise shade is important, ask if you can test before purchase.

Printed in Spain by Elkar S. Coop, Bilbao 48012.